DISASTER SCIENCE

AVALANCHES

BY NAOMI CAMERON

Gareth Stevens
PUBLISHING

Please visit our website, www.garethstevens.com. For a free color catalog of all our high-quality books, call toll free 1-800-542-2595 or fax 1-877-542-2596.

Cataloging-in-Publication Data
Names: Cameron, Naomi.
Title: Avalanches / Naomi Cameron.
Description: Buffalo, NY : Gareth Stevens Publishing, 2027. | Series: Disaster science | Includes glossary and index.
Identifiers: ISBN 9781482481983 (pbk.) | ISBN 9781482481990 (library bound) | ISBN 9781482482003 (ebook)
Subjects: LCSH: Avalanches--Juvenile literature.
Classification: LCC QC929.A8 C364 2027 | DDC 551.57848--dc23

Published in 2027
Gareth Stevens Publishing
2544 Clinton Street
Buffalo, NY 14224

Portions of this work were originally authored by Trudi Strain Trueit and published as *Detecting Avalanches*. All new material in this edition was authored by Naomi Cameron.

Designer: Joshua Olson
Editor: Claire Vanden Branden
Content Consultant: Jordy Hendrikx, Associate Professor of Geography, Snow and Avalanche Lab, Department of Earth Sciences, Montana State University

Photo Credits: Cover, p. 1 Marcus Placidus/Shutterstock.com; p. 4 Lex Nast/Shutterstock.com; pp. 7, 25 Ground Picture/Shutterstock.com; p. 8 Andrew Arseev/Shutterstock.com; p. 11 W. W. Webb/Shutterstock.com; p. 13 Vladimir Tretyakov/Shutterstock.com; p. 14 Juraj Kral/ Shutterstock.com; p. 16 Zuykov Photography/Shutterstock.com; pp. 18, 23 mcmortgreen/ Shutterstock.com; p. 20 mato/Shutterstock.com; p. 26 Bizi88/Shutterstock.com; p. 29 Dragos Asaftei/Shutterstock.com.

Printed in China

CPSIA compliance information: Batch #QS27GS: For further information contact Gareth Stevens at 1-800-542-2595.

TABLE OF CONTENTS

CHAPTER 1

DEADLY DISASTER

On March 4, 2025, a group of people were heli-skiing in Alaska. The skiers and their guide took a helicopter up the Chugach Mountains to ski a **remote** area. The guide went down first. He cleared a path for the other skiers to follow.

Three of the skiers started down the slope. Suddenly, a slab of snow broke away.

The Chugach Mountains are a famous place for people to hike and ski.

It was an avalanche on the mountain! The three skiers opened their safety airbags. But it was no use. They were buried under the snow. Their bodies were never found.

Approximately 150 people die in avalanches every year. Around 30 of those deaths happen in the United States.

HARD TO FIND

The area where the skiers got buried is very hard to get to. The ground is rough and steep. People can only go there by helicopter. Rescue teams also estimate that the skiers were covered by 40 to 100 feet (12 to 30 m) of snow. This made it hard for rescue teams to reach the skiers.

On average, people can be buried 4 feet (1.3 m) under the snow after an avalanche.

Scientists aim to understand when avalanches will happen. This way, they can help save lives.

CHAPTER 2

WARNING SIGNS

Every mountain snowfall adds another layer to the winter **snowpack**. Each layer of snow has its own texture, strength, and types of snow crystals. The weakest layer in the snowpack can spell trouble. Too much weight on top of it may cause it to break. Sometimes just one skier can do it. The slab slides downhill, taking all the snow above it.

Some avalanches travel 80 miles per hour (129 km/h) down a slope.

It picks up more snow on the way. An avalanche may weigh millions of pounds and travel as fast as a car on the freeway.

Avalanches almost always come with warning signs. People can learn to recognize these signs. A rapid rise in air temperatures is one such clue. This quick warming will melt snow, weakening the snowpack. Another concern is a storm that dumps several feet of new snow. This adds weight to the snowpack, increasing the avalanche threat. Snow already on the ground may pose a risk, too. Winds can move snow to other slopes and shape it into dangerous positions. A cornice is an overhang of snow on a ridge. Winds push

Areas with high avalanche risk may have road signs warning people of the possible danger.

snow into this position. A cornice can easily break off and trigger a slide.

Avalanche forecasters detect avalanche warning signs. They alert the public to danger. These experts post an avalanche **advisory** each day from winter through early spring.

Avalanche danger is ranked as low, considerable, high, or extreme. When the danger is rated high or extreme, avalanches are very likely to happen. Ski resorts and road crews check the stability in their own areas. They may use explosive charges to bring down dangerous masses

SNOW DETECTIVES

Avalanche forecasters typically have a degree in Earth sciences or engineering. Some work for a ski resort or an outdoor adventure company. Others work at highway departments, for their states, or at avalanche centers. Many avalanche centers across the United States are operated by the US Forest Service.

Experts can set off controlled avalanches by dropping explosives from helicopters.

of snow. Outdoor sports fans depend on local advisories to make safe decisions.

CHAPTER 3

WATCHING THE WEATHER

Nothing affects avalanche danger more than the weather. Snowfall and wind are responsible for creating and shaping the snowpack. Forecasters keep close watch on the skies. Weather in the mountains can change quickly.

Weather monitoring stations collect data to help create weather forecasts.

People traveling in snowy, mountainous areas must pay close attention to weather forecasts.

Forecasters may take manual weather observations. They use several instruments to do this. A thermometer measures snow and air temperatures. An **anemometer** detects wind speed.

A vane shows the wind direction. And a snow sampling tube gauges snow depth and density.

Most avalanche centers gather data from automated weather stations. The stations are placed on mountains. They measure temperature, wind speed and direction, and **precipitation**. They also measure humidity and snow depth. The stations regularly send data to computers at the nearest avalanche center.

The US Department of Agriculture runs a network of weather stations called SNOTEL. More than 800 of these stations collect information about snow and send it to scientists.

Avalanche forecasters take snow measurements to help determine what is safe.

Avalanche forecasters also receive regular weather forecasts and **satellite** images from the National Weather Service.

Satellites in space observe developing storms and track their movements. Images from the satellites allow scientists to estimate snow cover and snowfall accumulations.

Another tool forecasters rely on is Doppler radar. This technology measures motion within a storm. Doppler radar can detect wind speeds. It can also track the type and intensity of precipitation. It can gauge how far away the storm is and how fast it is moving. The National Weather Service operates a network of 160 Doppler radar systems across the United States.

inaer
PELIKAN 1
ELISOCCORSO PROVINCIALE

CHAPTER 4

SAFETY CHECKS

Many forecasters travel to mountains to examine the **terrain** and snowpack. They take safety equipment and a partner.

Avalanches tend to occur on mountain slopes steeper than 30 degrees. A tool called an **inclinometer** is used to measure the angle of a hill. Forecasters also note the placement of trees, bushes, and rocks.

People use helicopters to study avalanche areas and carry out rescues.

These objects act as anchors to help hold snow in place. However, they may also become dangerous in an avalanche. About one-quarter of avalanche victims in the United States die from hitting trees and other objects as they are swept downhill.

In the field, forecasters perform snow stability tests to detect weak layers. One method is called a shovel tilt test. This is best for the top layer of snow. The forecaster digs out a chunk of snow and picks it up with a shovel blade. Then the forecaster taps the blade's bottom. With each tap, the forecaster checks for any cracks in the snow.

Avalanche forecasters perform snow stability tests over many days to decide if snow is stable or not.

Another method is called a compression test. A forecaster digs a snow pit, leaving a column of snow. He or she places a shovel face down on top of the column. Then the forecaster begins tapping the shovel, completing three sets of ten taps. Each set

SOUNDS OF SURVIVAL

Someone buried beneath the snow has enough air to breathe for approximately 15 minutes. For this reason, an avalanche transceiver is an important tool for anyone heading into remote snowy areas. This small device can send and receive electronic signals. If a person is buried by an avalanche, his or her partners can turn on their transceivers. Then they'll receive the signal. Rescue teams can then track the signal, find the person, and dig the person out.

Rescue crews sometimes use dogs to help track down people buried by avalanches.

is harder than the one before it. Observing when the snow drops, breaks, or pops reveals how weak the layer of snow is.

Avalanche probes help rescuers find where to dig in the snow in order to rescue someone who is buried.

A similar technique is called the extended column test. It tests the snow's stability by checking a wider area. It provides information about how likely a crack in the snow is to spread.

These tests provide important information about how to stay safe. They can help inform travelers about which path to take on the mountain. But before taking that journey, mountain travelers should prepare by taking avalanche safety and rescue courses. These classes can be found across the United States.

In most avalanches involving deaths in the United States, the event was triggered by a person's movements. If properly prepared, skiers, adventurers, and explorers can recognize the signs of avalanches. They can use safety equipment to save many lives—including their own.

FACT FILE

AVALANCHE SAFETY

Before going up on a mountain, check local forecasts. Find out about any possible signs of danger. It's important to know what areas may be at risk. Some factors could trigger an avalanche, such as steep slopes or increased snowfall.

Also make sure you have the right equipment. Bring a transceiver, a shovel, and an avalanche probe. Make sure you have a partner, too. That way, if there is trouble, your partner is the first person who can help.

If you do get caught in an avalanche, yell for help. Then others will know where you are. If you find someone buried in the snow, dig the person out. Start slightly downhill so that the snow doesn't pack firmly around the person. Once you get the person out, provide first aid and keep them warm.

People can carry avalanche airbags in their backpacks as an added safety feature.

Also call 911. The **dispatcher** will send a rescue team to come help.

TEST YOUR KNOWLEDGE

Take this quiz to test your knowledge.

1. Write a sentence that describes the key ideas from Chapter 2.

2. Do you think the government should be responsible for providing avalanche forecasts to the public? Why or why not?

3. What weather condition commonly occurs before an avalanche?

    A. quickly warming temperatures
    B. quickly cooling temperatures
    C. temperatures that remain the same for a long time

4. Why do avalanches tend to occur on steep slopes?

    A. More snow falls on steep slopes.
    B. Temperatures are higher on steep slopes.
    C. The force of gravity pulls the snow down.

Answers can be found on page 32.

GLOSSARY

advisory
A public bulletin issued to warn of danger.

anemometer
An instrument for measuring wind speeds.

dispatcher
A person who takes emergency calls and works to send help.

inclinometer
An instrument for measuring the angle of a slope.

precipitation
Water that falls from clouds to the ground in the form of rain, hail, or snow.

remote
Far from towns or people.

satellite
A spacecraft that orbits Earth, often to collect information.

snowpack
The buildup of packed snow in a mountainous region.

terrain
The physical features of an area of land.

FOR MORE INFORMATION

BOOKS

Murray, Julie. *Avalanches.* Minneapolis, MN: Abdo Publishing, 2025.

O'Brien, Cynthia. *Mountain Survival Stories.* Minneapolis: Lerner Publications, 2026.

WEBSITES

Britannica Kids: Avalanche
kids.britannica.com/kids/article/avalanche/399351
Find out more about how and why avalanches happen.

National Geographic: Avalanches 101
education.nationalgeographic.org/resource/avalanches-101-wbt
Learn more fascinating facts about avalanches.

Publisher's note to educators and parents: Our editors have carefully reviewed these websites to ensure that they are suitable for students. Many websites change frequently, however, and we cannot guarantee that a site's future contents will continue to meet our high standards of quality and educational value. Be advised that students should be closely supervised whenever they access the internet.

INDEX

Answer Key: 1. Answers will vary; 2. Answers will vary; 3. A; 4. C